Vesuvius at Home

poems by

Jennifer Liou

Finishing Line Press
Georgetown, Kentucky

Vesuvius at Home

Copyright © 2017 by Jennifer Liou
ISBN 978-1-63534-200-0 First Edition
All rights reserved under International and Pan-American Copyright Conventions.
No part of this book may be reproduced in any manner whatsoever without written permission from the publisher, except in the case of brief quotations embodied in critical articles and reviews.

ACKNOWLEDGMENTS

"A Natural History" – published in the *Orange Coast Review*
"Cold Snap" – published in the *Orange Coast Review*
"Morning and Night" – published in the *Evergreen Review*
"My Dead Goat" – published in *Faultline*
"Preventive Medicine" – published in the *Adirondack Review*
"Shelter" – published in *Dirtcakes*
"Stealing Home" – published in *Literbug*
"Bitter Stalks" – published in *The Los Angeles Review*
"The Monastery at Ganagobie" – published in *Faultline*
"The Potbellied Stove" – published in *Faultline*
"Two Good Shoes" – published in *Zocalo Public Square*
"View from the Fortress of Sisteron" – published in *Faultline*
"We Would Have Washed Away" – published in the *Adirondack Review*

Publisher: Leah Maines

Editor: Christen Kincaid

Author Photo: Jennifer Liou

Cover Art: Libby Catchings

Cover Design: Elizabeth Maines McCleavy

Printed in the USA on acid-free paper.
Order online: www.finishinglinepress.com
also available on amazon.com

Author inquiries and mail orders:
Finishing Line Press
P. O. Box 1626
Georgetown, Kentucky 40324
U. S. A.

Table of Contents

- Bitter Stalks 1
- Preparations 2
- Birthday 3
- Our Bones 4
- We Would Have Washed Away 5
- A Natural History 6
- In the Doctor's Parking Lot 7
- Shelter 8
- Foundling 9
- Morning and Night 10
- The Potbellied Stove 11
- No Geodes 12
- Cold Snap 13
- Limpid Water 14
- Preventive Medicine 15
- Driving Home 16
- Two Good Shoes 17
- Insomnia Runs in the Family 18
- Deadheading 19
- The Monastery at Ganagobie 20
- View from the Fortress of Sisteron 21
- Les Calanques 22
- Divorce 23
- How I Used to Be 24
- Leaving 25
- My Dead Goat 26
- After the Funeral, Upstream 27
- Too Late 28
- Hard Water 29
- Aquifer 30
- Stealing Home 31

Volcanoes be in Sicily
And South America
I judge from my Geography
Volcanoes nearer here
A Lava step at any time
Am I inclined to climb
A Crater I may contemplate
Vesuvius at Home

—Emily Dickinson

Bitter Stalks

My dad and I drank Taiwan Beer
while my mom went to the zoo. It was a hundred degrees.
All week she announced that being here made my father wish
he'd married someone else. A fever seared his forehead, sealed his lips.
I told her she was crazy. His father died. He was grieving.
He was ill. I was wrong. We went on pointless errands—
found varnish for the table, plates to replace
the chipped ones in the set. The things you do to
anchor yourself in a city. All the street-side restaurants
overflowed. There for the choosing, I thought. I could have anything.
But we sat down and he ordered without pause,
familiar combinations, obeying life-long laws of bitter stalks,
scallops seared on impact, garlic sweetening slowly.
And he says he loved a girl, half a century ago.
He bicycled across the island
just to see her, through the lush steep hills of blue
and green hurtling towards extinction.
Her family turned him away. He moved to America.
So I was raised in a staunch white house where wheat
meets the unsatisfied sky. And when he leaves for work,
he hugs my mother so hard she complains. He's trying to
reshape her. I'm starting to think that's how it
always goes, or at least, I've inherited strong shoulders
and a question: Is this where infidelity begins—
an elsewhere mind, these unrelenting arms?

Preparations

My mother cried when her in-laws announced their visit.
In preparation, she instructed my father to trim the hedges.

A little off the left, a little off the right, top, bottom, right again.
Below the year's new growth, trapped detritus, scarecrow hands.

She cried. It was like the time, she said, my father taught her sparse Chinese,
took her shopping for gifts, packed her bags, trimmed her hair.

A little off the left, a little off the right... she cried. He took her home to
meet his parents. Nobody liked anyone else. Nobody liked her hair.

Dad says if I tie twine to a stick, prop a garbage can lid and wait,
I might catch a bird. He wants me out of the house. They need to get ready.

I lift a robin unexpectedly, traversing the lawns and curbs of Grant Street.
Bare hands, light breath sheathed in red, girl bent around her palms.

Birthday

On the phone, my father slips up, sends me love from
both his parents though it's just his mother now.
Planes weave the air carrying letters, their contrails signaling
numb heights and usual distances. He looks into the air above his garden
and the kitchen where my mother chops tomatoes with a dulling knife,
where they've replaced their table with a smaller table.

Our Bones

My father picks his mother's skull out of ashes
and we sort through the lesser bones

while he writes on her urn.
He's practiced weeks for this,

hiding a fever, hiding a shaky hand.
He wants us to mark this well.

We're here to learn about our family,
how the rice fields that were his are no one's now,

the brothers who were his—
marked with forgotten stones.

I saw the great fires.

I saw the sweat on his brow as he
hefted her into the oven then shut the door.

Is this the closest we can come to love?
Even the earth has no room for us,
so we make each other small.

We Would Have Washed Away

The first night we camped in a parking lot and set out early,
despite the warning signs, despite the rush of summer's
last snow raking the mountains.
She looks younger than my father, so it's not
just her growing old that's disconcerting. In the sequence we project,
my mother is my time machine, so I don't like looking
at her calves and knees above her boots.
We walked all day under the August sun
until we reached the river where the bridge was out.
She crossed on a fallen log, and I crossed on a fallen log
downstream, as if I could catch her.

A Natural History

Suet is fat and millet
stained in shades my mother likes
and birds don't seem to mind.

She kneads salt and flour,
homemade playdough, doles it out, doles out
buttons torn from her clothes.

Neighborhood children mold fanged sharks
and jellyfish and eels gleaming with
big, round plastic eyes.

Finally left alone, my mother traces
seascapes on the countertops.
children build their monsters,

songbirds crack their skulls against
windowpanes. Suet is fat and millet; my mother
feeds the birds and then picks up behind.

In the Doctor's Parking Lot

I let my father shop for me
because he needed something to shrink the time that
opens onto the universe when someone you love
might be dying.
After her appointment, he showed my new skirt to my mother.
Silk—it's silk, he said. Then added she'd have had one
too, if she'd been with us.
And it's not a garment I'm holding anymore—
it is her early absence
and my father's worry and my own
inability to tell the ones I love most that I do.
Wind gusts through the silk
making it dance, as if air were more flesh than I am.
C'mon, I say, let's get out of here.

Oh, our frantic, unreachable bodies.

Shelter

I could have married a man
who built planes, my mother said to me,
in the dead of noon, when we were alone
and a plane roared over our heads.

She said: I didn't have options like you will.

It was December. We still had months
until green heat poured grass into the hollows
and the lake ice started gnawing itself like a scab.

I was a child. I could still act
like I didn't know what she was talking about.

The reservoir was just a sheet of white.
I didn't think about the dam, the thwarted river.

Since then, when I grow restless, I focus on the weather.
Winter stills the water. It doesn't get presumptuous.

Algae grows beautifully beneath the daring crystals
and all the fish turn back into the depths.

In that lake world, which is mine, and my mother's
and my father's too, when we are calm and virtuous, and busy
pretending any of us know how to love,
the light and the cold are the same.

Foundling

When our sheepdog brought the newborn rabbit
to us in the cradle of his mouth,
my brother and I soothed its rumpled pelt
and sponged it dry. My mother said
without a hesitation: There's no use.
Is it that easy to jettison love? Love, she said
has nothing to do with it. That tiny plan
of a rabbit reeked of the world already, like hands
scheming sundering, the mouth of a beast
unearthing sanctuary. The rest must have followed
mercy's tired logic too, but the memory fades
before I decide what I am compelled to see done
with that heartbeat, already singled out
for loss, and this one, and this one, and this one, and this one.

Morning and Night

While my father's visiting his mother one last time,
mine, left home, is weaving a shell of busyness. Even from here,

I can help, our daily phone calls help. Leaving jars the dogs
from slumber every morning. Every night is spent in town—

she plays the recorder with friends. Or walks into theatres alone.
Wakefulness is a purse of artifacts—tickets, sheet music.

Their hours scarcely overlap but if she waits
late enough, he sometimes calls from his island of mist,

from his hour of calm before his mother and siblings
wake up and start fueling their diseases.

My mother's almost sleeping now.
Sleep will turn the day's events to an hourglass's sand,

pieces of the day too small to remember intact
that kept it from going unmarked. She'll remember tonight

she saw Jane Goodall speak in the steady, competent voice
that lulled everyone to sleep in the auditorium.

She'll remember what was spoken of: life spent in the midst
of necessary others, having halfway chosen such alliances.

The Potbellied Stove

The story goes your dog caught the rabbit that's been
simmering all afternoon. He licks the plates when we're done,
sprawling against your legs and one of mine.
That he can touch us both at once means we're
too close, we'd never hunch like this over the flame
if someone were watching
though it must be wonderful leaning where you'd like,
gleaning heat through layers of denim and wool.
I'm afraid we're the kind of people
who don't do what we should for others—
it's a distance we can talk across because it's never
personal, never a compromise. You're glad
she's coming to visit. You still can't explain why you left.
And I'm thinking of my husband, repeating the word.
I've caught myself red-handed
playing a child's game, saying the same thing over until it stops
making sense, stops reaching out to connect to what
might turn it into something
less lonely than itself. Please tell me
other thoughts are worse. I'm almost convinced.
Just think of our rabbit, neck snapped in the stew—
a meager body snared by accident
draining its blood into beets from the unthawed ground.

No Geodes

My head on your shoulder is the beginning of a life
in which worry sends you to sleep and keeps me awake.

Tell me things won't always be like this.
It will be summer soon. Then fall, frail but certain.

By then we'll be able to help each other survive.
I'll stop trying to gnaw you in half, having found someway to stop

being the child who smashes every stone to find out
within every stone is more stone.

Cold Snap

In Ozu's *Early Summer*, the daughter marries
and her father's household dissolves.
Not that she's caused anything; they had been waiting
to see her off before retiring to the country.
The bustling household echoes their last days together
back to them as if the house had grown,
anticipating solitude. I asked my parents to watch it.
They never bring it up, though they bring up
in various fashions, my leaving.
Of course I love this—my father's crisp
stomp up the driveway he just shoveled,
my mother's scraping my car windows.
And these words they repeat upon parting,
warnings and the offerings—their worries,
no, the names of their worries
lifting, calm bodies of fog.

Limpid Water

From the ridge-top there was no shore.
We saw only vibrant blue,
placid, not yet forced up into breakers,
and we paused to memorize the gorge,
clear blue all the way down.

Preventive Medicine

It's not that I'm averse to having my
nipples squeezed, or that I distrust
the plastic expertise of strangers.

She does it deftly, telling me to get all the
calcium I need by twenty seven.
I am to inspect myself every month

because small changes begin
a small, hungry death. My
longevity her first concern,

she does it all through gloves and then takes
off the gloves, bone-white fingers
caressing themselves under running water.

Driving Home

I think of my mother with her wrecked eye, her troublesome cysts,
waiting for me to call as we drop back down into the smog.
Out the passenger window, a figure grows into a young man
pushing a woman in a wheelchair uphill.
You're driving, love, so I'm not sure you see it.
And I catch myself practicing how I'll repeat this later.
She's quite old, a grandmother, at least,
whose weight he bears without effort.
She's happy, clutching flowers he brought, as they pass from sight
towards the young mountains.

Two Good Shoes

I'm worried about surviving
because it hasn't happened as we'd hoped.
I wanted the guilt of excess absolved
and it's doubled.

I don't want to be married anymore.

What is there to do
but call my mother who must know what it's like
because last time I called, she'd just the spent morning
gathering garbage, wind-strewn out of the can into the trees.

She'd thought she'd
done well, dealt with it already, as I sometimes
think she thinks of me. And now she's cleaning up
again.

She's worried she'll worry me with her complaints

because that's what her parents do.
They seem to live in mild but vocal suffering probably
beyond our imagining.

Their mistakes are indignations—
the one about Grandma working overtime at the Y,

earning money for two pairs of good shoes
then one day wearing one of each because
morning was dark and she hadn't been looking
and now she's looking.

Insomnia Runs in the Family

One night, my mother calls me
to say my father is suddenly old.
She woke up next to him, dismayed.

She says that every morning, now,
they take the dogs outside in darkness and

as he ascends the driveway towards her,
she sees his father's face in his,

 that latent family ghost.

I feel bad for her, I do, and for myself,
for all of us whose proxy for love
is the spectre of death in each other.

But when I can't sleep, I read
and drink, then walk down to waves
that I don't really care about.

All summer long,
there's been a seal on the beach
missing its head.

Sometimes the waves wash dead things up
and cannot wash them away.

You know it's true.
You know that's why we wear our rings less often,

and I don't say how much I dread and envy them, my parents,
who, after thirty three years of passionless truce, live

far from the sea, the whole weight of sky
pinning them down, together.

Deadheading

I wanted you to choose our avocados
because you're good at gaging ripeness, guessing the future.

I asked you to believe in my good clear heart
but the kitchen knife is truth and every vegetable

a body poised for betrayal. The apple is mealy, the avocado
brown, the pomegranate bruised beyond repair.

I've learned the sound of your car
idling for a moment in the driveway

before you walk in, seeking calm.
I wish I could be someone else for you,

someone who doesn't need love that wants to be torn down
like basil that lives if I keep it from blooming.

The Monastery at Ganagobie

I thought the tombs were troughs for watering sheep
until she climbed in and laid her white neck in the leaves. We're happy,
sacrilegious tourists posing for the camera in an empty grave.

Sierra flies to London.
And you and I, we fall into our old routines—coffee every morning,
books all afternoon. We find relief in silence and in our sense of breaking it,

descending to the cellar for a bottle, reading passages out loud.
Lonely for an unwelcome third to fend off worrying, we conjure her faults:
she's bossy in the kitchen, she patronizes us

although we need her deft French in the marketplace.
You won't be in any of the photographs. I'm the bellwether, weathervane,
barometer. Sunburnt at the beach, wind-whipped at the citadels.

And she's always posing, taking advantage of lightning,
occupying spaces emptied of their dead. After she leaves,
you erase the photographs in which she's

obviously prettier. We overeat,
drink for the drowsy haze, our way of anchoring ourselves
in the coarseness of our bodies, subjecting ourselves to the habits
that are making us the same.

View from the Fortress of Sisteron

And now we have to descend, so that the bathers
look as large as life again—

to where the village stops looking like a map of itself
to where the river is a barrier between the highway

and the households doing quiet commerce with the hills.
Already, we're negotiating absences, planning visits,

deciding how we'll spend the years we live apart.
After the last war, the castle lay in ruins, but it has been rebuilt.

The new walls are straighter than the rest, their mortar more secure,
the earth piled behind them held in check more steadily.

Old people have trouble with the stairs, but in great numbers
they lay siege to the citadel and ascend its terraced walks.

We descend at their speed, locked in step behind a wobbling couple,
while the earth nears and our vertigo gives way.

At the confluence of rivers, the town is ruined over and over.
Lowlands soothe the mountains. The rivers soothe the plains

but carry them away. Look down—for a moment the country is wild—
rocks
break though the hills, and the river hasn't plunged into the power plant.

Les Calanques

The guidebook led me to expect a rugged shoreline,
steep inlets permitting the deep sea's wild intrusion.

Yet I know butts and tits have lingered
where I'm sitting with my book,

which makes its windswept cleanliness deceptive.
We'll spend this year together then you'll leave.

I'm anticipating pristine loneliness,
lovely, austere faithfulness.

Try to imagine it from here, on this shore—
topless girls sunning their nipples from the rocks,

and in one gorge, a rainbow of plastic boats
thrashing the still water of the bay
into small blue wheat.

Divorce

This house is small
and full of echoes,
comforting. When something
goes wrong, I'll know.
But raising succor to his mouth,
he doesn't hear
the faint tug of mug and table
relinquishing each other.

How I Used to Be

The tree line is sudden as an argument
tracing some invisible divide
between enough and not enough. Here, a
hundred feet of brazen green and there,
bare earth, granite, alpine grasses pretending
they can set root without need. They need the
unapparent moisture, bright light of the refracted sun,
thin air, the wind, rivulets of snowmelt
stippling the trail. I prefer the gentle woods,
before this. Slow climbs and the fragrant duff,
the hair-pinned river which, compelled to move
onwards retraces as closely as possible
its old self—that cut-bank, point-bar river
refusing departure. Give me the thin line, the sliver.

Leaving

The flatland by the river, full of apple trees,
cedes mud to tarmac and sparkling cars.
Turn back here, let's not drive to the airport yet, though
I too have started dreaming of the jet's cool blast,
Marseilles made miniature and the grey-blue windswept seas.
Last week we ran through orchards,
past all the barricades. I remember feeling free
because they let us, they even waved us onward, saying
take what you can carry—your arms hold almost nothing.

My Dead Goat

When it died, they buried it in its layers of hair,
layers of gristle, in the assured airs of being loved
they had loved to laugh over. My family sunk it
in the outer pasture, beneath the un-culled small pines
shading the grass. Over it, they placed its former shed,
so returning to visit, I would imagine the goat
inside, in its usual place, not bother with inspection.
They wouldn't fear my apathy. I wouldn't risk
discovering I'd respond like that. And
no one, for now, would have any reason to say
of course this had to happen, you know that.

After the Funeral, Upstream

My father—
a fleck at the stern of the cruise ship.

The Yangtze River runs only one way, my uncle says—
great men and small men never return.

And yet the ship ascends. This way the trip takes longer,
the river doesn't spit us out

the way it would have before they cut it off.
Green cliffs close up behind us infidels who visit and leave.

There's a corpse outside our window and there's
no point trying to keep the dead in their graves.

My brother is the fat young ghost of my uncle. I'm
full-grown and I'm alone again, but that's

harder to address. This is unhealthy, my father says to me,
pinching the shoulder of his sleeping son.

You're squandering
everything, his forehead shouts in the mouths of its furrows.

You think at every turn you can go back,
lose those pounds, put on that wedding ring.

But now
my grandma's dead, burnt
until her bones fit through an oven grate,

and I still see my father at the stern of that boat
getting shut out of his country.

Too Late

It was hot and he was old so I stopped. Half his teeth were
perfect, the others missing. Two of his fingers were
blown off at the knuckles—he had been a miner. He had
been in fights and quoted Robert Service who said
each fresh move is only a fresh mistake.
Had I been young when he was young I would have found him
handsome, which was an unfair thought—he was telling me about
cancer. He described ranches we would pass
in canyons receding from the road—
fragrant grasses, soils washed down from streams…
The Ruby Mountains cast shadows in the foothills
laced with trails ascending past them.
Those trails all led to houses, and he wished one were his,
wished he had spent his life so as to allow it.

Hard Water

I'm finally glad you're gone. Confucius calls
taking hold of a clear concept "grasping
the azure." You left me to clean things up
again—polish on the steel, abrasives
on the tile—the work of erasing a life of things
getting dirty, breaking down. When I'm done
I shower once more in the empty house
in the tub I couldn't quite scrub clean.
We live in a mineral city. All the wrong things
accrete and accrue. Like loving you. Tell me:
why does what's left behind form rings bluer
than the sky, as if an ocean swelled
its banks in a time so distant that the land
and sea were different and everyone was happy?

Aquifer

My parents' conflicts shake the walls—
My mother's fever-pitch,
my father's resignation. God, I envy
how they stare each other down
when the dinner party fails,
when winter brings the flu,
when all their animals rebel.
Locked in confrontation, neither thinks to leave.
I learned that from them like I learned
how flame replenishes
the deep brown of the garden,
how willful agitation
brings ripe apples to the ground.
It hasn't worked for me.
The ones I've loved have fled.
My parents love geology as if it were the way
all this could end in ruin
and leave them innocent.
They'd leave each other but volcanic hills
conspire to make them stay
and so there's nothing to say
when my mother carries on like this
about our natural mysteries,
how when our water's gone, it's gone.
It fills her with a quiet thrill,
imagining the aquifer is going to abandon her
the way my father never will,
though maybe they would like that, both of them,
depleted love. Why can't I learn
that from my mother too, whatever makes her
secretly relieved when she observes
the storms are not enough,
those small reprieves,
rain in the smeared green hills—

Stealing Home

We haven't seen all of each other's wardrobes yet—
your merino wool and my silk dress— and probably we won't.
We're wedged next to the bar, agreeing

no one steals home anymore;
the pitcher's stretch guards against it.
There are less risky choices,

the sacrifice bunt, for example.
I've never followed baseball, though I remember
straining against the night

in a game where distances vanish first,
the fly ball at the top of its arc, the pitch
escaping the hand, until there's no

keeping your eye on the ball,
just the bat's crack and illuminated scramble
when cars turn down the block

worrying parents.
I'm sure kids still play ball on that street,
careless shouts piercing my parents' concerns over

me, single again, and when the porch lights
flood the streets with controlling love,
what must they think, unable to call me in from a game
in which I don't want to see beyond my hands?

Jennifer Liou lives multiple, simultaneous lives in rural Idaho, where she teaches, writes, cage fights professionally, does salmon preservation work for the Nez Perce Tribe, and explores the region's beautiful wilderness every chance she gets. She had an English PhD and creative writing MFA from the University of California, Irvine, and she has a biology degree as well. Her poems have appeared in numerous journals and she's currently working on a memoir about mixed martial arts.

www.ingramcontent.com/pod-product-compliance
Lightning Source LLC
LaVergne TN
LVHW041504070426
835507LV00012B/1325